WATERY WORLDS

POLAR SEAS

Jinny Johnson

W
FRANKLIN WATTS
LONDON • SYDNEY

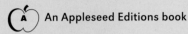 An Appleseed Editions book

Paperback edition 2015

First published in 2011 by Franklin Watts
338 Euston Road, London NW1 3BH

Franklin Watts Australia
Hachette Children's Books
Level 17/207 Kent St, Sydney, NSW 2000

© 2011 Appleseed Editions

Created by Appleseed Editions Ltd,
Well House, Friars Hill, Guestling,
East Sussex TN35 4ET

Designed by Hel James
Illustrations by Graham Rosewarne
Edited by Mary-Jane Wilkins
Picture research by Su Alexander

ISBN 978 1 4451 3829 9
Dewey Classification 577.6'3

A CIP catalogue for this book is available from the British Library.

Picture credits
t = top, b = bottom, l = left, right = right
Contents page Armin Rose/Shutterstock; 4 Photodynamic/Shutterstock; 5 Thomas Barrat/Shutterstock;
6 Wolfgang Poelzer/Photolibrary, 6/7 background Hunta/Shutterstock, 7t Paul Kay/Photolibrary, b
Herb Segars/Photolibrary; 8 David B Fleetham/Photolibrary, 8/9 background Gentoo Multimedia Ltd/
Shutterstock, 9t Christopher Meder-Photography/Shutterstock, b Michael S Nolan/Photolibrary; 10
Darla Hallmark/Shutterstock, 10/11 background Thomas Barrat/Shutterstock, 11t Peter Arnold Images/
Photolibrary, b Nik Nikiz/Shutterstock; 12 Mark Hamblin/Photolibrary; 13t Roger Eritja/Photolibrary,
c Ian Davies/Shutterstock, b Halldor Eiriksson/Shutterstock; 14 Gail Johnson/Shutterstock, 14/15
background Hunta/Shutterstock, 15t Thijs Schouten Fotografie/Shutterstock, b Antoine Beyeler/
Shutterstock; 16 Kim Westerskov/Alamy, 16/17 background Photodynamic/Shutterstock, 17t Doug
Allan/ Photolibrary, b Rick Price/ Photolibrary; 18 Blickwinkel/Alamy, 18/19 background Armin Rose/
Shutterstock, 19 Robert Harding Travel/Photolibrary; 20 Gentoo Multimedia Ltd/Shutterstock, 20/21
background Fred Hendriks/Shutterstock, 21t Chris Gomersall/Alamy, b Photodynamics/Shutterstock;
22 Rich Lindie/Shutterstock, 22/23 background Photodynamic/Shutterstock, 23t Richard Fitzer/
Shutterstock, b Worldswildlifewonders/Shutterstock; 24 Peter Arnold Images/Photolibrary; 25
WaterFrame-Underwater Images/Photolibrary; 26 Jan Martin Will/Shutterstock, 26/27 background
Fred Hendriks/Shutterstock, 27t Mogens Trolle/Shutterstock, b Ferderic B /Shutterstock; 29 Frank
Hurley/Photolibrary; 30/31 background Armin Rose/Shutterstock; 32 background Hunta/Shutterstock
Front cover: clockwise from top Fred Hendriks/Shutterstock, Mark Hamblin/Photolibrary, Nik Nikiz,
Mogens Trolle/both Shutterstock

Printed in China

Franklin Watts is a division of Hachette Children's Books,
an Hachette UK company.
www.hachette.co.uk

Contents

Icy worlds

The polar seas are the waters at the far north and south of the world – the Arctic and the Antarctic. These are the coldest places on Earth. Here it is so cold that even the seawater freezes over in winter. Then it is called pack ice.

Icebergs make good resting places for penguins.

You might be surprised to hear that many different animals live in the polar seas, despite the cold. There are billions of tiny creatures that are like shrimps and lots of fish, crabs and **squid**, as well as much larger animals such as whales and seals. Many birds also come to these icy oceans to find food.

Amazing!

Arctic sea ice can be three metres thick in some places. That's about as thick as 15 mattresses piled on top of one another!

A polar bear and her cub trek across the pack ice in search of food. Polar bears often have to travel long distances to find prey.

WATCH OUT!

Strong ocean **currents** and winds take polluting chemicals from all over the world to the Arctic. The **pollution** these chemicals cause is worse in the Arctic than in the countries where the chemicals are made.

Arctic fish

At least 240 different kinds of fish swim in the Arctic Ocean. There are Arctic cod and Arctic char, as well as fish called eelpouts, sculpins and flatfish.

Many of the fish live near the bottom of the sea. They feed on **plankton** – tiny animals floating in the water – as well as other fish and sea creatures. Then seals and whales eat the fish.

The female Arctic cod lays just one batch of eggs in her life. This can contain as many as 11,500 eggs.

Amazing!

Arctic char spend winter in the sea, but swim into rivers to lay their eggs.

Guess what?

The right-eye flounder is a flatfish that lives in the Arctic Ocean and spends most of its time on the seabed. It is born with an eye on each side of its head. Gradually the left eye moves to the right side so the fish can see as it lies on the seabed.

The polar eelpout lives on seabeds, and looks for worms and other small creatures to eat.

Whales in the Arctic

The narwhal has one big tusk at the front of its head. This is actually a very long tooth.

Amazing!

Lots of different kinds of whale live in the Arctic. Humpback whales arrive in the summer to feed on the shrimp-like krill and small fish that live in the polar sea. In winter the whales travel to warmer waters near the equator. Here they mate and give birth to their young.

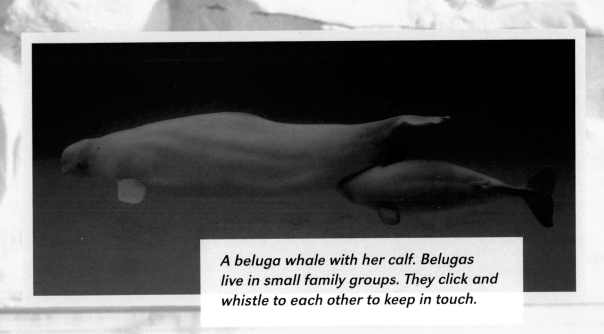

A beluga whale with her calf. Belugas live in small family groups. They click and whistle to each other to keep in touch.

The beluga whale and the narwhal live in the Arctic all year round. In winter most of the sea is frozen over. Then the whales have to find holes in the ice where they can come to the surface to breathe. They eat fish, squid, shrimp and other sea creatures.

WATCH OUT!

The bowhead is another whale that lives in the Arctic. It is rare because so many were killed by whalers in the past. Now the bowhead is an **endangered species**.

Humpback whales leap out of the water and then crash back down. No one knows why they do this – it might be just for fun!

Polar bears

Polar bears live in the Arctic. They are the biggest bears in the world and are also called 'sea bear' because they spend so much time in or near the sea. They are very good swimmers and find their food in the sea.

Ringed and bearded seals are the main prey of polar bears, but they also hunt bigger animals such as walrus and beluga whales.

Under its white fur, a polar bear's skin is black.

Amazing!

When swimming, a polar bear uses its front paws as paddles and steers with its back paws.

A polar bear watches by a seal's breathing hole. It finds the hole by smell.

In the winter most of the sea is frozen over, so the bears can move around on the ice easily. They search for breathing holes where seals pop up to take a breath of air. A bear will lie in wait near a hole, ready to pounce when a seal appears.

WATCH OUT!
The world's changing **climate** means that there is less sea ice today in the Arctic during the summer. This makes it harder for bears to move around and find enough food.

Arctic birds

Only a few kinds of bird stay in Arctic waters all year round. The little auk and ivory gull both do. The ivory gull catches fish to eat, but it also follows polar bears and gobbles up what is left of their kills.

Many birds fly north to the Arctic for the summer. Skuas, puffins and guillemots all do this. There is lots of food for them in the Arctic during the warmer months. The Arctic tern also goes to the Arctic in summer. It flies all the way from Antarctica, where it lives when it is summer there and while it is winter in the Arctic.

The little auk flies fast and can also swim under water to catch tiny sea creatures and small fish.

Guess what?

The Arctic skua is a flying pirate! This big seabird steals food from other birds. It attacks birds such as terns and gulls as they carry food to their nests, and forces them to drop their catch.

The pure white ivory gull makes its nest on Arctic coasts and lays up to three eggs.

The little Arctic tern flies about 71,000 kilometres every year as it travels between the Arctic and Antarctic.

Amazing!

Walrus

The huge walrus is a type of seal with long tusks, like an elephant. It lives in Arctic seas, but often hauls itself out of the water to lie on pack ice. The body of a walrus is covered with a thick layer of fat, called **blubber**. This keeps the walrus warm in cold sea and on the ice.

A walrus mainly eats clams, but it also feeds on worms, squid and other sea creatures. It dives down and feels around with the sensitive **bristles** on its nose. These bristles

The walrus's tusks are really huge teeth, which grow up to a metre long.

Amazing!

A walrus can swim at 35 km/h for short distances, but its normal swimming speed is about 7 km/h.

help the walrus find food on the seabed. A walrus can stay under water for up to ten minutes before it has to come to the surface to take a breath.

Guess what?
The walrus has a big appetite. It can eat as many as 6,000 clams in one go.

Walrus often use their long tusks to haul themselves out of the sea.

Antarctic fish

Some very unusual fish live in Antarctic waters. They manage to live in the coldest area on Earth and they have special ways of surviving the freezing temperatures.

The Antarctic cod has a long sleep in winter, like a kind of **hibernation**. It stays close to the seabed and its heartbeat slows right down while it sleeps. From time to time, the cod wakes up and eats just enough food to stay alive.

A Weddell seal catches an Antarctic cod.

Amazing!

The icefish is the
only vertebrate (an animal
with a backbone) that does not
have red blood. Its blood
looks almost clear.

Another amazing
creature is the icefish.
Its body contains a
substance which stops
it freezing in the very
cold water.

WATCH OUT!

Fishermen catch fish such
as the Patagonian toothfish
in the sea around Antarctica.
Sometimes their fishing lines
also accidentally catch and
kill many seabirds.

Krill – food for many

Antarctic krill are a kind of shrimp. A krill is about five centimetres long and weighs only a gram, but there are billions of them. They are probably the most important animals that live in Antarctic waters.

Krill feed on tiny plants that float in the water. These plants are called phytoplankton and are so small you cannot see them without a magnifying glass. There are lots of them in the Antarctic seas so there is plenty of food for krill. Many different creatures eat the krill in turn – fish, birds and the enormous blue whale.

A blue whale eats about 40 million krill a day.

Amazing!

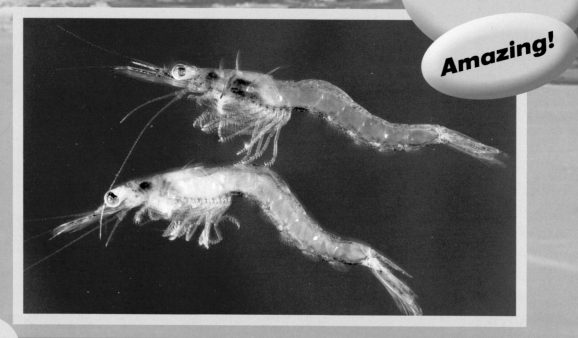

Guess what?
Scientists think that there are so many krill that together these little creatures might weigh more than all the people in the world.

This swarm of krill has been turned pink by the heat made by volcanoes erupting in Antarctica.

Penguins

Penguins are the most common birds in Antarctica. The emperor and the Adélie penguins spend their whole lives on and around the icy continent, while the gentoo and the chinstrap breed on islands nearby. Penguins have wings but cannot fly.

Penguins use their wings like flippers to speed through the water. They spend a lot of time in the sea, where they catch fish, squid and other small sea creatures. A penguin's body is covered with a thick layer of fatty blubber which keeps it warm under its waterproof feathers.

Emperor penguins are the largest of all the penguins. They can be 1.2 metres tall – that's taller than most nine-year-olds.

Amazing!

A penguin can swim at 25 kilometres per hour – much faster than a human can swim. Even the fastest Olympic champion can only swim at eight kilometres per hour.

WATCH OUT!

There are plenty of penguins in Antarctica today, but if **global warming** continues and the temperature rises, life will become difficult for them. More sea ice will melt and it will be harder for the penguins to find enough food and places to nest.

A penguin holds its feet neatly against its body and flaps its paddle-like wings as it swims. This is a gentoo penguin.

Chinstrap penguins breed in huge colonies on Antarctic islands.

Elephant seals

The southern elephant seal, which lives in Antarctica, is the largest seal in the world. The male weighs as much as an elephant and is longer than a family car. This seal gets its name from the male's large trunklike nose.

This giant, like other seals, is a **mammal** and not a fish. It spends most of its life in the water, but comes to the surface to breathe. It dives very deep to find fish and squid to eat and can stay under water for an amazing two hours.

Male elephant seals have very big noses.

A male elephant seal behind a smaller female. Females give birth to one pup each year.

Guess what?

Southern elephant seal pups are born in the Antarctic summer and grow quickly before winter starts. They feed on their mother's rich fatty milk. By the time they are three weeks old they weigh three times more than when they were born.

Male elephant seals fight one another for the right to mate with females.

Squid and other creatures

Invertebrates are animals which don't have a backbone. Lots of them live in Antarctic waters. These include huge spider crabs, starfish and many kinds of squid.

Squid are related to snails and slugs, but they look very different. A squid has a long bag-shaped body, eight arms lined with **suckers** and two long tentacles for catching prey. A squid bites its prey with its sharp beak.

Red starfish live in Antarctic waters. Here one is attacking a sea urchin. Starfish also eat sea sponges and seal poo!

Guess what?

Antarctic sea spiders are amazing creatures related to spiders and crabs. A sea spider has mouthparts which look like a drinking straw. It sticks them into its prey and sucks out the body juices.

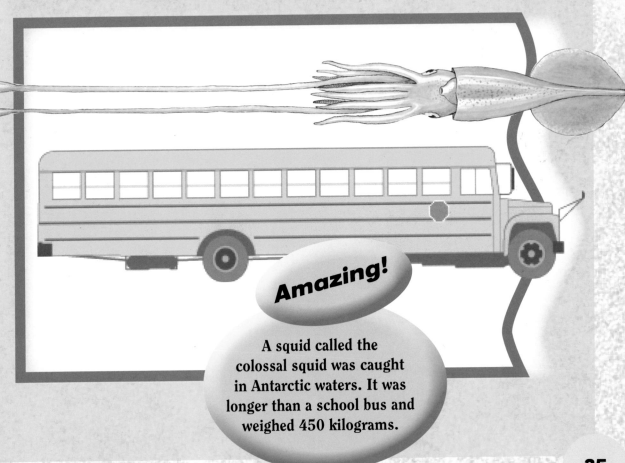

Amazing!

A squid called the colossal squid was caught in Antarctic waters. It was longer than a school bus and weighed 450 kilograms.

Antarctic hunters

The leopard seal is one of the fiercest hunters in Antarctic waters. It moves fast and can see and smell very well. It also has long sharp teeth. Penguins are its main prey, but it also eats fish, squid and other seals.

The only hunter that can outwit the leopard seal is the killer whale. These whales live in all seas but there are lots of them around Antarctica and not many creatures can escape them. Killer whales sometimes hunt in groups and scientists have seen them nudging floating ice to tip the seals lying on top of it into the water.

Leopard seals have long sharp teeth and strong jaws for killing their prey.

WATCH OUT!

Today, Antarctica is too cold for sharks, but if the waters get just a few degrees warmer because of global warming sharks might move in. This would mean big changes for other wildlife in the area.

The leopard seal has a thick layer of blubber to keep it warm.

Amazing!

The teeth of a killer whale can be ten centimetres long.

Killer whales, or orca, eat more than 200 kilos of food a day.

World oceans: Southern

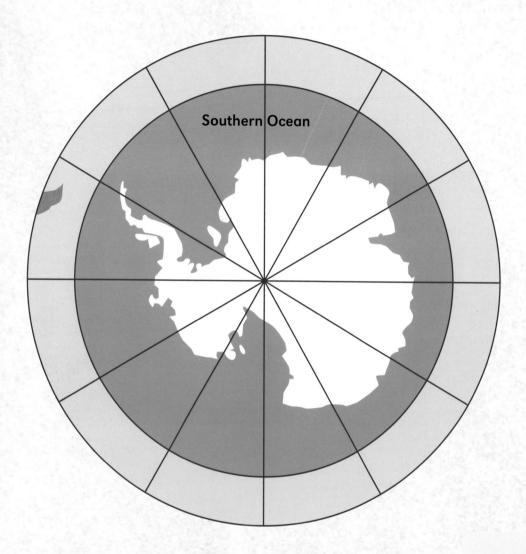

Southern Ocean

In 2000 scientists decided that the southern parts of the Atlantic, Indian and Pacific oceans should be called the Southern Ocean. The Southern Ocean is the fourth largest of the world's oceans. It covers an area which is about twice the size of the United States.

The Southern Ocean totally surrounds Antarctica.

Southern Ocean facts

The Southern Ocean is very deep. Most of it is 4,000-5,000 metres deep and there are few shallow areas.

The water at the deepest point is 7,235 metres deep.

In winter, ice forms on the sea around Antarctica. By the end of the winter the ice makes the continent twice as big as it is in the summer.

Huge icebergs drift around the Southern Ocean. You can usually see just one-eighth of an iceberg above the water.

The world's biggest ocean current is in the Southern Ocean. It flows around the continent of Antarctica.

Ernest Shackleton made four trips to Antarctica. In 1914, his ship Endurance was trapped in the ice. Shackleton and some others had to make a dangerous journey to find help. Amazingly, everyone survived.

Watery words

blubber
A layer of fat covering the body of a marine mammal such as a seal. The fat helps to keep the animal warm.

bristles
Short stiff hairs on an animal's nose.

climate
The weather – temperature, rain, snow, wind – in a particular area.

current
The movement of water.

endangered species
Types of animals and plants that may become extinct – disappear for ever.

global warming
The increase in temperature of the Earth's atmosphere.

hibernation
A sleep-like state in which some animals pass the winter months.

icebergs
Icebergs are large pieces of ice that break off glaciers or ice shelves. Most of an iceberg is below the surface and you can only see the top.

invertebrate
An animal without a backbone. Worms, shrimp and crabs are all invertebrates.

mammal
A warm-blooded animal that feeds its young with milk from its body. Land mammals have four legs but sea-living mammals, such as whales, have flippers.

plankton
Tiny plants and animals that live floating in water. Many other animals feed on plankton.

pollution
The introduction of things that damage the natural world, such as litter and oil.

prey
An animal that is hunted and eaten by another animal.

squid
An animal with a long body like a bag, eight arms and two longer tentacles.

suckers
Cup-shaped parts on the tentacles or arms of some animals, which can cling on to things.

vertebrate
An animal with a backbone. Mammals, birds, reptiles, amphibians and fish are all vertebrates.

Index